EVERYDAY
SOUTHERN
FAVORITES

120 Tasty Recipes

BARBOUR
PUBLISHING

© 2010 by Barbour Publishing, Inc.

Compiled by Laura Demse.

ISBN 978-1-61626-015-6

Cover image: S Lee Studios/Fresh Food Images/Photolibrary

Published by Barbour Publishing, Inc., P.O. Box 719, Uhrichsville, Ohio 44683, www.barbourbooks.com

Our mission is to publish and distribute inspirational products offering exceptional value and biblical encouragement to the masses.

 Member of the
Evangelical Christian
Publishers Association

Printed in China.

INSPIRATION
at your fingertips!

Looking for a simple way to bring new life to your kitchen? This book is for you. Within these pages, you'll find dozens of tasty recipes that are filled with Southern charm and hospitality and are a delight to share with family and friends.

Finding a recipe is as easy as flipping through the book. At the bottom of each page, you'll see a color that corresponds to one of five categories:

So set up this little book on your countertop, flip page after page for good-eatin' inspiration and kitchen tips and tricks, and you might just find a little encouragement for your soul along the way. *Ya'll enjoy!*

BREADS

He will cover you with his feathers.
He will shelter you with his wings.
His faithful promises are your armor
and protection.
PSALM 91:4

CAST-IRON SKILLET CORNBREAD

4 cups cornmeal
2 teaspoons baking soda
2 teaspoons salt
4 eggs, well beaten
4 cups buttermilk
½ cup melted butter

....

Combine dry ingredients. Add eggs and buttermilk; mix well. Stir in melted butter. Heat a well-greased 10½-inch cast-iron skillet in a 400-degree oven for 3 minutes or until very hot. Pour batter into hot skillet. Bake at 450 degrees for 40 minutes or until golden brown.

SPOON BREAD

3 eggs, well beaten
1 tablespoon melted butter
⅔ cup white cornmeal
¼ teaspoon baking soda
1 teaspoon salt
¼ cup sugar
2 cups buttermilk

....

Preheat oven to 425 degrees. Combine eggs and melted butter. In a separate bowl, combine dry ingredients. Add to egg mixture alternately with buttermilk; mix well. Bake 45 minutes in a buttered 1½-quart baking dish. Serve hot.

PETE'S BERRY MUFFINS

2 cups prepared baking mix
½ cup sugar
1 egg
⅔ cup milk
1 tablespoon melted butter
1 cup fresh or frozen berries (blueberries, blackberries, raspberries, or dewberries)

....

Mix dry ingredients into a large bowl. Gently mix in the egg, milk, and melted butter until just combined. Fold in berries. Fill buttered or paper-lined muffin tins ⅔ full and bake at 400 degrees for 15 to 20 minutes. Yield: 1 dozen

RICE MUFFINS

1 cup flour
1 tablespoon sugar
1 teaspoon baking powder
½ teaspoon salt
2 eggs
½ cup cream or milk
4 tablespoons melted butter
1 cup cooked rice

....

Preheat oven to 375 degrees. Sift dry ingredients into a large bowl. Make a hole in the center of the ingredients and add the eggs, cream, and melted butter. Mix all together until just combined. Fold in rice. Fill buttered or paper-lined muffin tins ⅔ full and bake 12 to 15 minutes. Yield: 1 dozen

RACHEL'S PINEAPPLE-PECAN LOAF

¾ cup brown sugar, packed
¼ cup shortening
1 egg
2 cups flour
1 teaspoon baking soda
½ teaspoon salt
⅓ cup frozen orange juice concentrate, thawed
1 cup crushed pineapple with juice
½ cup chopped pecans

....

Cream together sugar and shortening; add egg and beat well. Sift dry ingredients, and add them to the creamed mixture alternately with the orange juice concentrate, stirring after each addition. Stir in pineapple with juice and pecans. Bake in a well-greased 9x5x3-inch loaf pan at 350 degrees for 50 to 60 minutes. Remove from pan and cool on rack before slicing. This bread freezes well.
Yield: 1 loaf

CANDACE'S APPLE BREAD

3 eggs
1 cup canola oil
1¾ cups sugar
½ teaspoon salt
2 cups flour
1 teaspoon cinnamon
1 teaspoon baking soda
1½ cups apples, cored, peeled, and chopped
¾ cup pecan or walnut pieces

Beat together eggs, oil, and sugar. Sift dry ingredients and combine with wet ingredients. Fold in apples and nuts. Bake in a greased 9x5x3-inch loaf pan at 350 degrees for 40 to 60 minutes or until pick in center comes out clean. Cool before slicing. Yield: 1 loaf

SWEET POTATO BISCUITS

1 ¼ cups self-rising flour
2 teaspoons brown sugar, packed
⅓ cup shortening
1 egg, beaten
½ cup mashed sweet potato
2 tablespoons milk

....

Stir dry ingredients together in a large bowl. Cut in shortening until mixture resembles coarse crumbs. Combine egg, sweet potato, and milk; add to dry ingredients. Stir until dough just clings together. Knead gently on lightly floured surface, about 10 strokes. Pat or roll dough to ½-inch thickness. Cut with biscuit cutter and place on greased or parchment-lined baking sheet. Bake at 425 degrees for 10 to 12 minutes. Yield: 8 biscuits

HANDY CONVERSIONS

1 teaspoon = 5 milliliters
1 tablespoon = 15 milliliters
1 fluid ounce = 30 milliliters
1 cup = 250 milliliters
1 pint = 2 cups (or 16 fluid ounces)
1 quart = 4 cups (or 2 pints or
32 fluid ounces)
1 gallon = 16 cups (or 4 quarts)
1 peck = 8 quarts
1 bushel = 4 pecks
1 pound = 454 grams

Quick Chart

Fahrenheit	Celsius
250°–300°	121°–149°
300°–325°	149°–163°
325°–350°	163°–177°
375°	191°
400°– 425°	204°–218°

JAM TWISTS

2¼ cups self-rising flour
4 tablespoons shortening
⅔ cup milk
Jam of choice

Put flour in a bowl and cut in shortening to resemble coarse crumbs. Stir in milk. Turn dough onto floured board and knead ½ minute. Roll to ¼-inch thickness. Cut dough into strips 3 inches long and 1 inch wide. Spread jam on half the strips, top with remaining strips. Twist and place on parchment-covered baking sheet. Bake at 375 degrees for 20 to 25 minutes. Yield: 16 twists

PERFECT PANCAKES

2 cups flour
2 teaspoons baking powder
1/4 teaspoon salt
3 egg yolks, beaten
2 cups milk
1/2 cup butter, melted
3 egg whites, beaten until stiff

Sift together dry ingredients in a large bowl. Add beaten egg yolks, milk, and melted butter, mixing well. Fold in stiffly beaten egg whites. Fry on a lightly greased hot griddle or skillet, turning once. Yield: about 30 pancakes

WONDERFUL WAFFLES

2 cups flour
4 teaspoons baking powder
1 tablespoon sugar
½ teaspoon salt
3 egg yolks, beaten
2 cups cream or milk
½ cup water
3 egg whites, beaten until stiff
3 teaspoons butter, melted

••

Sift together dry ingredients in a large bowl. Add beaten egg yolks, milk, and water, mixing well. Fold in stiffly beaten egg whites and then butter. Bake in a preheated waffle iron, following manufacturer's instructions. These waffles should be crisp on the outside and tender inside.

CHEESE BISCUITS

2 cups flour
4 teaspoons baking powder
1 teaspoon salt
2 tablespoons butter, softened
¾ to 1 cup milk
¾ cup grated cheese (American or cheddar)

....

Sift together dry ingredients in a large bowl. Cut butter into dry ingredients with pastry blender. Gradually stir in milk and cheese until stiff dough forms. Roll gently on floured board to ½-inch thickness. Cut out biscuits and place on parchment-lined baking sheet. Bake at 425 degrees 10 to 15 minutes.

DATE NUT BREAD

1½ cups boiling water
1½ cups dates, cut into pieces
1 tablespoon butter
1 cup sugar
1 egg, beaten
1 teaspoon vanilla
2¼ cups sifted flour
½ teaspoon baking soda
½ teaspoon salt
1 cup nuts, chopped

....

Pour boiling water over dates and let set until cool.
Cream butter and sugar; add egg and vanilla. Add dates
and water alternately with combined dry ingredients.
Add nuts. Pour mixture into a well-greased 9x5x3-inch
loaf pan. Bake at 325 degrees for 1 hour and 15 minutes.
Top should feel firm when done and pick in center
should come out clean. Slice when cool. Yield: 1 loaf

NO-KNEAD WHOLE-WHEAT BREAD

⅔ cup warm water (100 degrees)
4 teaspoons dry yeast
2 teaspoons honey
5 cups whole-wheat flour
3 tablespoons molasses combined with
  ⅔ cup warm water
1⅓ cups boiling water
⅓ cup wheat germ
1 teaspoon salt
1 teaspoon sesame seeds

....

Combine ⅔ cup water, yeast, and honey. Heat flour
for 20 minutes in 250-degree oven. Add yeast mixture
to molasses water. Stir into warm flour. Add 1⅓ cups
boiling water, wheat germ, and salt. Dough will be sticky.
Turn dough into greased 9x5x3-inch loaf pan. Sprinkle
with sesame seeds. Let rise in warm place 40 to 60
minutes. Bake in preheated 425-degree oven for 50
minutes. Yield: 1 loaf

RYE BREAD

2 cups lukewarm water
2 teaspoons salt
¼ cup shortening
¼ cup molasses
2 tablespoons sugar
2 teaspoons dry yeast
3 cups rye flour
2 cups flour

....

Mix all ingredients together in a large bowl. Knead
on a lightly floured board for about 5 minutes; add
more flour if necessary to prevent sticking. Put dough
in greased bowl, cover with towel or plastic wrap to
rise in warm place until double in size. Punch down
dough, divide in half, and form two
loaves. Turn each loaf into
a greased 9x5x3-inch
loaf pan. Cover and
let rise in warm
place until risen
2 inches. Bake at
350 degrees for 35
minutes. Yield: 2 loaves

REFRIGERATOR ROLLS

2 packages active dry yeast
2 cups warm water
½ cup sugar
2 teaspoons salt
¼ cup shortening
1 egg
6½ to 7 cups flour

....

Dissolve yeast in water in a large bowl. Stir in sugar, salt, shortening, and egg. Mix flour in by hand until dough is easy to handle. Place in refrigerator for at least 3 hours; may be kept in the refrigerator for up to 3 days. Shape dough into rolls about 2 hours before baking. Let rise in warm place until double in size. Bake at 400 degrees for 12 to 15 minutes.

SCOOP IT UP!

Squeeze-handle scoops, like those used to dip ice cream, come in a variety of sizes that range from 2 teaspoons to ⅔ cup. This makes them perfect for many tasks, including shaping cookies and candies, neatly scooping chicken or tuna salads, or to fill muffin tins easily. Large scoops can even be used to make individual meat loaves.

············· **Quick Tip** ·············

CARAWAY BLUE CHEESE PUFFS

1 (8 ounce) tube refrigerated buttermilk biscuits
3 tablespoons caraway seeds
⅓ cup butter, melted
1 (4 ounce) package blue cheese crumbles

....

Remove biscuits from tube and cut each into quarters.
Roll each into a ball and then roll in caraway seeds that
have been spread thinly on flat dish. Place balls in a
13x9-inch baking dish. Combine melted butter and blue
cheese in a small saucepan. When combined, pour over
rolls. Bake at 425 degrees for 10 minutes.

LEMONY MUFFINS

3 cups flour
2 teaspoons baking powder
1 teaspoon salt
2⅔ cups sugar, divided
1 cup canola oil
1 cup milk
3 eggs
1 teaspoon vanilla
Juice and zest of 1 lemon
⅓ cup lemon juice
Crystal sugar for topping, optional

....

Combine flour, baking powder, and salt. In another bowl combine 2 cups sugar, oil, milk, eggs, vanilla, and lemon juice and zest from lemon. Combine wet and dry ingredients without overmixing. Fill buttered or paper-lined muffin tins ⅔ full. Bake at 350 degrees for 25 to 35 minutes. Combine ⅔ cup sugar and ⅓ cup lemon juice in saucepan. Heat to boiling and until sugar is dissolved. Brush or spoon syrup over each muffin until absorbed. Sprinkle with crystal sugar. Yield: 20 muffins

HUSH PUPPIES

2 cups white cornmeal
1 tablespoon flour
½ teaspoon baking soda
1 teaspoon salt
1 egg, beaten
3 tablespoons onion, finely chopped
1 cup buttermilk

....

Mix dry ingredients in a large bowl. Add egg, onion, and buttermilk. Mix well and drop by tablespoonfuls into deep hot oil that is at 360 degrees to 375 degrees. When they float they are done. Remove from oil and drain. Serve hot. Yield: 20 to 25 hush puppies

SOUTHERN CREAM BISCUITS

2 cups flour
2 teaspoons baking powder
$\frac{1}{2}$ teaspoon salt
4 tablespoons cold butter, cut into pieces
1 cup heavy cream

Preheat oven to 450 degrees. Blend dry ingredients into a large bowl. Cut in the butter until the mixture resembles coarse crumbs. Add cream a little at a time, while tossing the mixture with a fork until a soft dough forms. Turn dough onto a lightly floured board and roll out $\frac{1}{2}$-inch thick. Cut out $2\frac{1}{2}$-inch biscuits. Bake the biscuits on ungreased baking sheet for 10 to 12 minutes or until golden brown. Yield: 1 dozen

LORI'S MAYONNAISE BISCUITS

2 cups self-rising flour
2 tablespoons mayonnaise
1 cup milk
2 tablespoons sugar

....

Preheat oven to 450 degrees. Mix ingredients together with a spoon. Spoon into greased muffin tins or onto greased baking sheet. Bake for 8 to 10 minutes, or until golden brown. Yield: 1 dozen

SKILLET BISCUITS

½ cup milk
2 tablespoons melted butter
1 tablespoon vinegar
½ teaspoon onion salt
1½ cups prepared biscuit mix
½ cup yellow cornmeal
2 tablespoons vegetable oil

....

Blend milk, butter, vinegar, and salt. In another bowl,
combine biscuit mix and cornmeal. Stir in liquid mixture
with a fork until dough forms a ball. On floured board,
knead 10 times. Shape into 1½-inch balls. Flatten with
your hand to ¼-inch thickness. In skillet, heat oil on
medium-low heat. Add biscuits. Cook until lightly
browned on both sides and cooked through. Add more
oil to skillet if necessary.

ONION SESAME BISCUITS

1 (8 to 10 count) tube refrigerator biscuits
1 large onion, chopped
1 tablespoon butter
1 teaspoon sesame seeds
½ teaspoon kosher or sea salt

....

Separate biscuits and place on baking sheet. Fry onion in butter until soft and then divide evenly onto top of each biscuit. Sprinkle sesame seeds and salt on top. Follow baking directions of biscuit package.

CRESCENT ROLLS

½ cup butter
5 tablespoons sugar
½ cup boiling water
1 egg, well beaten
1 package yeast
½ cup cold water
Dash salt
3 cups flour

....

Cream butter and sugar; add boiling water and let cool.
Add egg. Dissolve yeast in cold water. Combine salt and
flour. Mix all ingredients together. Cover and refrigerate
overnight. Divide dough in half. Roll each half to ¼-inch
thickness and 12 inches long. Cut into 16 wedges. Roll
up starting at rounded edge. Place on baking sheet with
point underneath. Let rise in a warm place about 3
hours. Bake at 400 degrees for 20 minutes.

TASTIER BREAD AND ROLLS

Enhance a plain roll or slice of bread with extra flavor. Soften a stick of butter then whip in your choice of garlic, rosemary, lemon juice, or honey.

Quick Tip

POPOVERS

1 ½ cups flour
¼ teaspoon salt
2 eggs, lightly beaten
1 ½ cups milk
2 tablespoons butter, melted

....

Preheat oven to 425 degrees. Sift together dry
ingredients. Blend in liquid ingredients to make a smooth
batter, beating for 3 minutes. Grease and heat muffin
cups in oven before filling. Fill muffin tins ⅔ full and bake
about 30 minutes. Do not open the oven until popovers
are puffed and golden brown. Yield: 1 dozen

STARTERS, SAUCES, SOUPS & SALADS

Always be full of joy in the Lord.
I say it again—rejoice!
PHILIPPIANS 4:4

SPICED ROASTED ALMONDS

1 egg white
1 teaspoon salt
2 teaspoons cumin
1 teaspoon cayenne pepper
2 teaspoons smoked Spanish or Hungarian paprika
2 cups blanched almonds

•••

In a bowl, whisk together egg white and seasonings.
Add almonds and toss to coat. Spread almonds evenly
on baking sheet and roast at 350 degrees for about 20
minutes, or until golden brown. Transfer to a rack to
cool before serving.

ORANGE WALNUTS

1½ cups sugar
½ cup orange juice
1 teaspoon grated orange rind
½ teaspoon vanilla
3 cups walnut halves

....

In saucepan, combine sugar and orange juice. Cook to
240 degrees or soft ball stage on candy thermometer.
Remove from heat; stir in orange rind, vanilla, and
walnuts. Stir until syrup begins to look cloudy; before
the mixture hardens, spoon onto waxed paper. Separate
nuts and let cool. Yield: about 1 pound

SALSA SPICE MIX

1½ cups dried cilantro or parsley
1½ teaspoons garlic powder
½ cup dried chopped onion
¼ cup dried red pepper flakes
1 tablespoon salt
1 tablespoon black pepper

....

Combine ingredients and store in an airtight container at room temperature. If you don't like cilantro, substitute dried parsley; the flavor will be different, but still very good.

To make Spicy Salsa: Blend 2 tablespoons mix with 1 (10 ounce) can Mexican-style tomatoes. Serve with chips or vegetables.

To make Salsa Spread: Blend 2 tablespoons mix with 1 cup softened cream cheese. Serve with crackers or as sandwich spread.

As a rub for meat: Rub spice mix on poultry or beef before roasting or grilling.

MANGO SALSA

1 mango, peeled, pitted, and chopped
¼ cup red bell pepper, finely chopped
1 green onion, chopped
2 tablespoons cilantro, roughly chopped
1 jalapeño pepper, finely chopped
2 tablespoons lime juice
1 tablespoon lemon juice

....

Combine ingredients. Cover and allow flavors to combine for at least 30 minutes before serving. This salsa can be served with poultry, fish, shrimp, or with tortilla chips.

AVOCADO SALAD

1 avocado, diced
1 red bell pepper, diced
1 yellow bell pepper, diced
½ red onion, diced
¼ cup fresh cilantro, roughly chopped
¼ cup olive oil
1 lime, juiced
⅛ teaspoon ground cumin
Kosher or sea salt and black pepper to taste

Mix ingredients thoroughly. Serve on lettuce or romaine leaves. Serves 6

RED PEPPER MARMALADE

6 red bell peppers, seeded and coarsely chopped
¾ cup sugar
¾ cup vinegar
Juice and zest of 1 orange
1 tablespoon jalapeño pepper, minced
Kosher or sea salt and black pepper to taste

....

Combine ingredients except salt in a nonreactive
saucepan. Simmer over low heat until marmalade
reaches a syrupy consistency, about 45 minutes; season
to taste. Remove from heat and chill before using. This
marmalade is excellent with poultry or as an appetizer
on top of cream cheese and served with crackers. Yield:
3 cups

SAUSAGE AND CHEESE DIP

1 pound bulk breakfast sausage
1 (8 ounce) package cream cheese
1 (16 ounce) jar black bean salsa

....

Cook sausage in skillet, stirring frequently, so sausage crumbles. Drain excess fat. Add cream cheese and heat on low heat until it melts into sausage. Add salsa. Continue heating until thoroughly warmed. Serve with tortilla or corn chips.

MONEY-SAVING TIP

Nonstick baking sprays are very convenient, but can be costly. You can save money by making your own nonstick baking mixture. Place 2 tablespoons each of flour, canola oil, and vegetable shortening in a bowl. Whisk ingredients together until they are fluffy. Store in an airtight container at room temperature. Stir before using; use wax paper or a pastry brush to apply lightly to baking pans.

Quick Tip

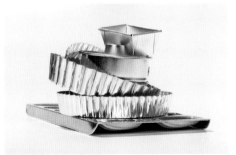

BASIC PESTO

2 cups fresh basil
2 cloves garlic, peeled
¼ cup pine nuts, toasted at 400 degrees for 10 minutes
½ teaspoon salt
1 teaspoon freshly ground black pepper
½ cup extra-virgin olive oil
¼ cup grated Parmesan cheese

....

Place all ingredients except olive oil and Parmesan into food processor. Pulse 2 to 3 minutes until ingredients are combined. While machine is running, slowly add oil, scraping side often with a spatula. Blend until a smooth, creamy paste. Remove pesto to a bowl and stir in cheese. Pesto can be used to top pasta or rice, or to flavor meat, soups, and sauces. Yield: about 2 cups

FRESH TOMATO SAUCE

2 pounds ripe plum tomatoes
1 small onion, finely minced
1 carrot, grated
1 stalk celery, minced
2 cloves garlic, minced
4 tablespoons extra-virgin olive oil
1/8 teaspoon hot pepper
2 tablespoons chopped fresh basil
Salt and pepper to taste

Blanch tomatoes in boiling water for 2 minutes; plunge into ice water, drain, and peel. Chop and set aside. In a 6-quart pot, sauté onion, carrot, celery, and garlic in oil until onion is transparent, about 5 minutes. Add tomatoes and hot pepper. Cook at medium heat for 20 minutes, until reduced. Add basil, salt, and pepper and cook for 10 minutes. Yield: 3 to 4 cups

FROZEN FRUIT SALAD

2 cups sour cream
¾ cup sugar
2 tablespoons lemon juice
1 (9 ounce) can crushed pineapple
1 banana, sliced
¼ cup chopped nuts
¼ cup chopped maraschino cherries
12 to 15 romaine lettuce leaves

....

Combine all ingredients except romaine leaves in a large bowl. Divide equally into ramekin dishes or cupcake tin cups. Freeze until solid. Remove salad from molds. Place romaine leaf on a plate and place salad on top before serving. Yield: 12 to 15 salads

BLACK BEAN SALAD

1 (16 ounce) can black beans, drained
1 (16 ounce) can sweet corn, drained
1 green bell pepper, chopped
1 red onion, chopped
1 cup cherry or grape tomatoes, halved if necessary
Scant 1/4 cup Italian or buttermilk ranch–style salad
   dressing

....

Combine all ingredients in a large bowl. Cover and
refrigerate until cold.

GAZPACHO

2 (16 ounce) cans whole tomatoes, undrained
2 cucumbers, peeled and cut into chunks
2 medium onions, quartered
4 garlic cloves, halved
2 red bell peppers, cut into chunks
1 green bell pepper, cut into chunks
½ cup fresh lemon juice
Salt and pepper to taste
Sour cream or plain yogurt

....

Combine ingredients (except
sour cream) in blender
and mix until thick.
Cover tightly and
chill overnight.
Serve in chilled
bowls. Garnish
with a dollop
of sour
cream or
yogurt.

FRESH MUSHROOM SOUP

2 quarts cold water
2 cups mushrooms, washed and sliced
1½ cups celery, diced
⅓ cup parsley, chopped
1 teaspoon salt
⅓ cup small noodles (orzo or alphabets)
1 small onion, chopped
⅓ cup butter
⅓ cup flour

In a large pot, bring first five ingredients to a boil; simmer for 15 minutes. Add noodles and simmer for 30 minutes. Brown onion in butter, remove onion and add to soup; save butter. Make a roux by whisking flour into butter, mixing until there are no lumps and flour starts to turn golden brown. Stir roux into soup while it is boiling; cook for 5 minutes before serving.

SPLIT PEA AND HAM SOUP

1 pound split green peas
Cold water to soak peas
1 ham bone
1 bay leaf
1 potato
1 carrot
1 large onion stuck with 6 cloves
2 large garlic cloves, mashed
Few peppercorns
2 quarts water
1 cup diced ham
Seasoned croutons

....

Soak peas in cold water to cover overnight; drain when ready to use. Put all ingredients except diced ham and croutons into a large pot. Bring to a boil; then simmer for 4 hours. Remove ham bone and bay leaf; put soup through sieve. Add diced ham. Sprinkle croutons over soup before serving.

COLD RED BEET SOUP

2 (16 ounce) cans sliced beets with juice
2 large cucumbers
4 cups milk
1 small onion, minced fine
4 sprigs dill, minced fine
2 cups water
¼ teaspoon salt
3 tablespoons vinegar
12 ice cubes
Sour cream or plain yogurt, optional

Dice beets and cucumbers. Place into bowl with beet juice and milk. Add onion and dill. Stir in water, salt, and vinegar. Add ice cubes and let stand. Serve cold. Garnish with a dollop of sour cream or yogurt, if desired.

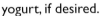

BAKING SPILL PICKUP!

When measuring dry ingredients, chances are
you'll wind up with a mess on your countertop.
Do your measuring over a paper plate or
a sheet of waxed paper. Spills can then be
picked up easily and returned to the canister,
preventing waste and making cleanup easier.

BRUSCHETTA WITH HERBED GOAT CHEESE

1 French baguette, sliced in ½-inch thick slices
3 tablespoons olive oil
⅓ cup fresh parsley, chopped
2 tablespoons fresh thyme, chopped
1 tablespoon fresh rosemary, chopped
2 teaspoons lemon zest
1½ teaspoons fresh ground black pepper
¼ teaspoon salt
1½ tablespoons extra-virgin olive oil
1 (11 ounce) log soft fresh goat cheese

....

Preheat oven to 375 degrees. Arrange the bread slices on large baking sheet. Drizzle with 3 tablespoons olive oil. Bake until golden and crisp, about 10 minutes. In a bowl, combine herbs, seasonings, and oil. Gradually add cheese, 2 teaspoons at a time. Spread on warm bread and serve at once.

ORANGE SHERBET SALAD

1 (6 ounce) box orange gelatin
2 cups boiling water
1 pint orange sherbet
1 (11 ounce) can mandarin oranges, drained
1 (20 ounce) can crushed pineapple, drained

••

Dissolve gelatin in boiling water. Stir in sherbet until melted. Add fruit and chill until firm.

MARGARET'S SUMMER SALAD DRESSING

1 cup oil
4 tablespoons cider vinegar
4 tablespoons lemon juice
4 teaspoons sugar
2 teaspoons Hungarian sweet paprika
2 teaspoons prepared mustard
1 teaspoon salt

....

Combine oil, vinegar, juice, sugar, paprika, mustard, and salt in a jar; shake until well mixed. Refrigerate until needed.

Serve over mixed greens, tomatoes, green beans, cucumber, or hard-cooked eggs. Be creative! Add tuna, shrimp, leftover cooked meat, pasta, or your favorite vegetables to the mix.

SHREDDED CARROT SALAD

1½ pounds carrots, peeled and grated
1 cup crushed pineapple, drained
1 cup mayonnaise or yogurt
1 cup raisins
½ cup powdered sugar
½ cup chopped pecans

....

Combine all ingredients. Cover and refrigerate until ready to serve.

TOMATO ASPIC

1 teaspoon fresh basil, chopped
2 cups tomato juice
1 (3 ounce) package lemon gelatin
2 tablespoons garlic vinegar
½ teaspoon salt
Crisp salad greens
4 teaspoons mayonnaise
Paprika

Add basil to tomato juice in saucepan and bring to boil.
Remove from heat and let cool 10 minutes; then strain.
Add gelatin, vinegar, and salt, stirring to dissolve. Pour
into individual salad molds or ramekin dishes. Chill.
Before serving, unmold aspic onto plated salad greens.
Top each with a teaspoon of mayonnaise and sprinkle
with paprika.

CORN SALAD

4 cups frozen corn
6 small mangoes, peeled, pitted, and roughly chopped
2 pounds jicama, peeled and chopped
1 cup red onion, chopped
½ cup fresh cilantro, roughly chopped
½ cup fresh lime juice
Salt and black pepper to taste

Combine first 6 ingredients in a large bowl. Season to taste with salt and pepper. Cover and refrigerate until cold for best flavor.

CAULIFLOWER SALAD

1 head lettuce
1 red onion
1 head cauliflower
1 pound bacon, fried and cut into small pieces
2 cups mayonnaise
⅛ cup sugar
1 cup Parmesan cheese, grated

Chop lettuce, onion, and cauliflower into bite-size pieces. Layer all ingredients into serving bowl in order given. Refrigerate until ready to use. Stir all together just before serving. This salad can be made the night before.

OLIVE SALAD

1 (16 ounce) jar salad olives, drained
1 (16 ounce) can medium whole black olives, drained
1 cup extra-virgin olive oil
⅛ teaspoon garlic powder
⅛ teaspoon crushed red pepper
⅛ teaspoon dried sweet basil
⅛ teaspoon dried oregano

....

Combine all ingredients. Cover and refrigerate
overnight. The olives can be eaten as a salad on mixed
greens or as an addition to your favorite salad.

FRESH VS. DRIED HERBS

There is nothing like using fresh herbs when cooking and baking, especially if they come from your own garden. However, if a recipe calls for fresh herbs and you only have dried available, use 1 teaspoon of dried leaf herbs or ½ teaspoon dried ground herbs for 1 tablespoon of chopped fresh herbs called for in the recipe.
If a recipe calls for any amount of a dried herb and you have it available as a fresh herb, double the amount of herb called for in the recipe.

Quick Tip

PIMENTO CHEESE

1 cup cheddar cheese, grated
1 cup mayonnaise
1/4 cup chopped pimento
1/8 cup sweet pickle relish
1/8 teaspoon horseradish

....

Combine all ingredients in a large bowl. Cover and refrigerate. Wonderful with fresh vegetables or as sandwich spread.

MAIN DISHES

*The generous will prosper;
those who refresh others will
themselves be refreshed.*
PROVERBS 11:25

BAKED FRIED CHICKEN

1 cup dry bread crumbs
½ cup Parmesan cheese
1 teaspoon basil
½ teaspoon oregano
½ teaspoon black pepper
¼ teaspoon seasoned salt
1½ pounds boneless chicken breasts
½ cup buttermilk

....

Preheat oven to 375 degrees. Grease the bottom of a baking sheet. In a shallow bowl, mix together crumbs, cheese, and seasonings. Coat the chicken with the buttermilk. Roll chicken in the seasoned bread crumb mixture. Place on the greased baking sheet. Bake for 20 minutes and then turn over the chicken pieces. Bake another 20 to 30 minutes, or until chicken is done and the juices run clear.

GARDEN CLUB CHICKEN CASSEROLE

2 cups celery, diced
1 cup onion, diced
1 can water chestnuts, drained and diced
3 tablespoons butter
3 cups cooked chicken, diced
2 cups cooked rice
1 (10.75 ounce) can condensed cream of chicken soup
1½ cups mayonnaise
1 cup crushed buttery crackers
½ cup slivered almonds
2 tablespoons butter, melted

....

In large skillet, sauté celery, onion, and water chestnuts in butter until tender. Combine with chicken, rice, soup, and mayonnaise, mixing gently. Place in 3-quart baking dish. Combine crackers, almonds, and melted butter. Sprinkle on top of casserole. Bake at 350 degrees for 40 minutes or until top is slightly browned. If prepared in advance, refrigerate and bake at 350 degrees for 1 hour.

CALLIE'S CHICKEN AND DUMPLINGS

3 pounds chicken pieces
1/4 teaspoon poultry seasoning
2 cups self-rising flour
1 egg
1 (10.75 ounce) can condensed cream of chicken soup

....

In large pot, cover chicken with water, add seasoning; bring to a boil. Cover; simmer 60 minutes. Remove chicken; let cool. Cut meat into bite-size pieces, discarding bones, skin; add meat back to the pot. Cover.

Mix flour, egg, 1 cup of broth, and enough water to make stiff dough. Knead dough on lightly floured board; roll until thin. Cut into 2-inch squares.

Bring broth to boil; add soup. Drop dumplings in. Do not stir while dumplings cook; shake the pot instead. Cook until boiling and the noodle-like dumplings rise to the top.

CARROLL'S EAST TEXAS SQUIRREL DUMPLINGS

3 to 4 red or grey squirrels*, dressed, cut up, salted,
   and peppered
⅛ cup shortening
3½ cups flour

....

In large pot, cover squirrel with 3 quarts water; bring to
boil. Cook until tender. This will take longer for older,
larger, or red squirrels. Keep broth at steady boil.

Cut shortening into flour, add 1 cup broth to make
stiff dough. The dough texture should be like piecrust
dough. Knead on lightly floured surface; roll until thin.
Cut into strips 1½ inches by 3 inches. Drop dumplings
into pot. Lower heat and continue stirring. Cook until
dumplings rise to the top.

*In East Texas, these squirrels are known as Cat
Squirrels or Fox Squirrels.

CORN CHIP CHILI PIE

2½ cups corn chips, divided
1 large onion, chopped
1 cup grated cheddar cheese, divided
1 (15 ounce) can chili without beans, heated

Place 2 cups corn chips in deep baking dish. Arrange onion and ½ cup cheese over the chips. Pour heated chili over ingredients in baking dish. Top with remaining corn chips and cheese. Bake at 350 degrees for 10 minutes or until cheese is melted.

GREENS AND HAM

½ pound ham with bone
¼ pound salt pork
1 medium onion, diced
2 teaspoons sugar
1 tablespoon chicken bouillon
3 pounds greens, cleaned, stems removed, chopped

··

Put all ingredients except greens in large pot; cover with water and bring to a boil. Cook for 30 minutes before adding greens. Cook an additional 30 minutes. Remove ham, dice meat, and return it to greens. Cook down until liquid is almost gone. Serve with cornbread. Kale, Swiss chard, turnip, mustard, or collard greens work well in this recipe.

PORK STEAKS AND HOMINY

4 pork steaks
1 clove garlic, minced
1 teaspoon salt
½ teaspoon thyme
¼ cup water
1 (16 ounce) can diced tomatoes, undrained
¼ cup flour
1 (16 ounce) can hominy
½ to 1 (4 ounce) can green chili peppers, drained

....

Brown pork steaks slowly on both sides. Pour off drippings. Sprinkle garlic, salt, and thyme over steaks; add water. Cover and cook on low heat for 30 minutes. Remove steaks. Drain and reserve liquid from tomatoes; combine liquid with flour in skillet and cook, stirring constantly, until thickened. Stir in tomatoes, hominy, and peppers. Place steaks on top. Cover; continue cooking about 15 minutes.

EASY CLEANUP

Cleaning up a greasy mess doesn't have to be a chore if you use this little trick: Sprinkle a generous amount of baking soda into your pan when you are done cooking; add a bit of water and blend to form a paste. Let your pan stand while you and your family enjoy a meal together. When you are ready to wash your pan, it will clean up fast. You won't believe the shine! (This little cleaning tip also works wonders on the stove top.)

Quick Tip

SHEPHERD'S PIE

2 tablespoons oil
1 small onion, diced
2 cups beef or lamb, cooked and diced
1 (10 ounce) package frozen mixed vegetables,
  slightly thawed
1 cup brown gravy
1/4 teaspoon marjoram
Salt and pepper to taste
2 cups mashed potatoes
1 egg, beaten

....

Heat oil in a 1 1/2-quart casserole and cook onion until
softened. Add meat, mixed vegetables, gravy, marjoram
and seasonings. Bring to a simmer. Combine mashed
potatoes and egg; pile around edges of casserole. Bake at
425 degrees for 20 minutes, until potatoes are browned.
Any cooked vegetables can be used in place of the
package of frozen mixed vegetables. Yield: 4 servings

POTATO AND SMOKED SAUSAGE BAKE

½ cup butter, melted
1 cup hot milk
3 eggs
3 pounds potatoes, peeled and grated
1 pound smoked sausage or kielbasa, cut in half
    lengthwise then cut into ½-inch pieces
Salt and pepper to taste

....

Combine liquid ingredients. Stir in potatoes and sausage.
Transfer to a lightly greased 9x13-inch baking dish. Bake
at 325 degrees for 1½ hours.

TUNA PASTA CASSEROLE

1 can (10.75 ounce) condensed cream of mushroom soup
2 tablespoons half-and-half or milk
1 (7 ounce) can tuna, drained and flaked
¼ cup chopped red pepper or pimento
⅛ teaspoon tarragon
4 ounces small shell pasta, cooked per package instructions and drained
1½ cups frozen peas
4 tablespoons seasoned stuffing mix, crushed
2 teaspoons butter, melted

....

In a large bowl, combine soup, half-and-half, tuna, red pepper, and tarragon. Fold in prepared pasta and peas. Spoon mixture into a lightly greased 1½-quart casserole dish. Combine stuffing mix with melted butter and sprinkle over top of casserole. Bake uncovered at 400 degrees for 35 minutes or until hot.

TILAPIA WITH GARLIC AND ONION

4 tilapia fillets
4 cloves garlic, crushed
1 large onion, chopped
1 teaspoon salt
1/8 teaspoon black or cayenne pepper
4 tablespoons olive oil

....

Place fish in shallow glass dish. Top the fillets with garlic, onion, salt, and pepper. Spoon the olive oil evenly over the top. Cover; refrigerate overnight or at least for 4 hours.

To Bake: Preheat oven to 350 degrees. Transfer fish and marinade to greased 9x13-inch baking dish. Bake for 30 minutes, or until fish flakes when touched with a fork.

To Grill: Wrap fish and marinade in aluminum foil and grill until done, about 30 minutes, or until it flakes when touched with a fork.

SAUSAGE GRAVY WITH BISCUITS

1 pound sausage
2 tablespoons sausage drippings or butter
2 tablespoons flour
4 cups milk, warmed
½ teaspoon black pepper
Baked biscuits

Brown and cook sausage thoroughly. Remove to bowl,
reserving drippings. Scrape up bits of sausage stuck
to pan. Whisk flour into hot drippings until smooth.
Add milk, stirring constantly, until thick and hot. Stir in
sausage and pepper. Serve over hot biscuits.

HAM WITH RED-EYE GRAVY

1 (¾-inch thick) country ham steak
2 tablespoons brown sugar
1 cup black coffee

....

Slash the edges of the ham steak to prevent curling. Fry ham in skillet on low heat until browned on one side, about 5 minutes. Turn the ham over and brown the second side. After ham is browned, remove to a platter and keep hot. Add brown sugar and coffee to the skillet, stirring to loosen any bits of ham stuck to the skillet. Bring to a boil, stirring occasionally; reduce by half. The gravy should be rich reddish-brown in color. Pour over ham and serve immediately.

UNSTUFFED CABBAGE

2 pounds ground beef
1 envelope dry onion soup mix
1 cup rice
1 can diced tomatoes
1 (10.75 ounce) can condensed tomato soup
2 soup cans water
2 pounds cabbage, shredded

....

In a large skillet, brown the beef with the onion soup mix. Add rice, tomatoes, tomato soup, and water. Place cabbage in casserole dish. Pour meat mixture over cabbage. Cover and bake at 325 degrees for 1 to 1½ hours, stirring occasionally.

AFTER CHURCH BEEF STEW

2 to 2½ pounds beef, cubed
1 teaspoon salt
1 teaspoon rosemary
¼ teaspoon black pepper
2 onions, roughly chopped
4 carrots, peeled and roughly chopped
2 stalks celery, roughly chopped
4 potatoes, peeled and cubed
1 (16 ounce) can diced tomatoes
1 (10.75 ounce) can condensed tomato soup
1 soup can water

....

Place beef in Dutch oven. Top with seasonings and vegetables. Combine soup and water and pour over ingredients to coat. Cover and bake at 300 degrees for 3 to 4 hours.

EASY PRODUCE CLEANING

To remove germs from fresh produce, spray with a mixture of ⅓ cup water and ⅔ cup white vinegar then rinse with fresh water. For best results, wash fresh produce just before you are ready to prepare it for serving.

JACKIE'S SLOPPY JOE OR CHILI SUPPER

1 large onion, chopped
1 green bell pepper, chopped
2 stalks celery, chopped
2 tablespoons oil
3 pounds ground meat (beef, turkey, or sausage)
1 (10.75 ounce) can condensed tomato soup
½ soup can water
1 (16 ounce) bottle chili sauce
1 (16 ounce) can red kidney beans (optional, for chili)

....

Sauté onion, bell pepper, and celery in oil until the onions are transparent. Place the ground meat into the same pan and cook until well browned. Add tomato soup and water; stir in the chili sauce. Add kidney beans at this point, if making chili. Simmer 30 minutes before serving.

SWEET & TANGY BARBEQUE CHICKEN

1 ½ tablespoons olive oil
¼ cup diced onion
2 cloves garlic, minced
5 tablespoons ketchup
3 tablespoons honey
3 tablespoons brown sugar
2 tablespoons apple cider vinegar
1 tablespoon Worcestershire sauce
Salt and pepper to taste
2 skinless, boneless chicken breast halves

Preheat grill for medium-high heat. Heat olive oil in a skillet over medium heat. Sauté onion and garlic until tender. Stir in ketchup, honey, brown sugar, apple cider vinegar, Worcestershire sauce, salt, and pepper. Cook for a few minutes to thicken sauce. Remove from heat, and allow to cool. Lightly oil the grill grate. Dip chicken in sauce, and turn to coat. Cook on grill for 10 to 15 minutes, turning once. Move chicken to the skillet with sauce. Simmer over medium heat about 5 minutes on each side.

MACARONI BROCCOLI AND CHEESE

1 (8 ounce) box elbow macaroni
1 cup fresh broccoli florets
1 tablespoon each olive oil and butter
2 tablespoons flour
2½ cups milk
¾ teaspoon salt and freshly ground black pepper
¾ cup each cheddar and Parmesan cheese, grated
¼ cup dry seasoned bread crumbs
¼ cup butter, melted

....

Cook macaroni in boiling water for 3 minutes; add broccoli, cook for 3 more minutes. Drain. In large skillet, heat oil and butter. Whisk in flour until there are no lumps; stir in milk. When hot, add salt, pepper, and cheeses. Mix in macaroni and broccoli. Pour into 9x13-inch baking dish. Combine bread crumbs and butter; sprinkle evenly over top. Bake at 400 degrees for 30 minutes.

ORANGE CHICKEN

1 egg
⅓ cup orange juice
1 to 1½ cups herb-seasoned stuffing mix, crushed
1½ teaspoons paprika
1 tablespoon grated orange zest
1 teaspoon salt
8 boneless, skinless chicken breasts
6 tablespoons butter, melted
1 orange, cut into 8 slices for garnish

In a bowl, beat egg and juice. In another, combine stuffing mix, paprika, zest, and salt. Dip chicken in egg mixture, then into crumbs, coating well. Pour half the melted butter into a 9x13-inch baking dish. Place chicken in dish and pour remaining butter on top. Bake uncovered at 375 degrees for 45 minutes, or until juices run clear.

GUACAMOLE BURGERS

1 pound ground beef
½ cup crushed corn chips
⅓ cup milk
1 teaspoon Worcestershire sauce
½ teaspoon onion powder
2 ripe avocados, pitted and mashed
2 tablespoons lemon juice
¾ teaspoon salt
½ onion, chopped
1 tomato, chopped
½ to 1 (4 ounce) can green chili peppers, drained
Toasted sandwich buns

....

Mix together first 5 ingredients and shape into 4 or 5 patties. Grill over hot coals about 4 to 5 minutes or until done. Combine remaining ingredients and spoon over grilled burgers in toasted buns. The guacamole can be made ahead of time. Reserve the avocado pit and put it in the guacamole to help prevent darkening. Cover the dish and refrigerate. Remove avocado pit before serving.

SCALLOPED HAM AND POTATOES

1 (2 pound) package hash brown potatoes
2 cups yellow onion, chopped
1/4 teaspoon salt
1/8 teaspoon black pepper
5 cups ham, diced
1/2 cup mushrooms, sliced
1 (10.75 ounce) can condensed cream of celery soup
1 cup sour cream
1 cup cheddar cheese, grated
1/4 cup Parmesan cheese, grated
1/4 cup dry unseasoned bread crumbs

....

Layer potatoes and onion in 3-quart baking dish. Sprinkle with salt and pepper. Top with ham and mushrooms. In a bowl, combine soup, sour cream, and cheddar cheese. Spoon over casserole. In a bowl, combine Parmesan and bread crumbs; sprinkle over top. Bake uncovered at 375 degrees for 50 to 55 minutes.

TURKEY RICE CASSEROLE

3 pounds turkey pieces
½ cup butter, melted
1 cup uncooked rice
2 cups milk
1 (10.75 ounce) can condensed cream of mushroom
 soup
1 (10.75 ounce) can condensed cream of celery soup
¼ teaspoon black pepper
1 envelope dry onion soup mix

....

Dip turkey pieces in melted butter and place in 9x13-inch baking dish. Pour remaining ingredients, except onion soup mix, over turkey. Sprinkle onion soup mix evenly over top. Cover and bake at 350 degrees for 2 hours.

CHERYL'S NOODLES WITH SMOKED SAUSAGE AND SHRIMP

½ cup each chopped onion, celery, green pepper
1 tablespoon olive oil
1½ teaspoons Italian seasoning
½ teaspoon crushed red pepper
½ pound smoked or andouille sausage, cut in half
  lengthwise then cut in ½-inch pieces
½ pound large shrimp, peeled and deveined
4 cups chicken broth
8 ounces angel hair pasta

··

In a large skillet, brown the onion, celery, and green pepper in olive oil over medium-high heat. Stir in seasonings, sausage, and shrimp. Cook 2 minutes, or until shrimp turns pink. Add broth and bring to boil. Break pasta in half and add to skillet. Cook 3 to 5 minutes or until pasta is done.

HANDY CONVERSIONS

Dried to Cooked Beans

1 cup of most dried beans =
2¼ to 2½ cups cooked
1 cup of dried chickpeas, lima, or great
northern beans = 2½ to 3 cups cooked beans
1 cup of dried lentils = 3 cups cooked

Quick
Chart

LYNDA'S TEXAS BUTTERBEAN BAKE

1 pound ground beef
2 onions, chopped
1 ½ cups tomato paste
¼ teaspoon ground dried mustard
¼ teaspoon thyme
¼ teaspoon oregano
½ teaspoon Worcestershire sauce
Salt and pepper to taste
½ teaspoon brown sugar
2 (16 ounce) cans butterbeans, drained

....

Brown the meat and onions. Mix in paste, seasonings, and brown sugar. Stir in beans. Transfer to greased casserole dish. Bake at 350 degrees for 45 to 60 minutes. The casserole should be just moist, not watery.

VEGETABLES, FRUITS & SIDE DISHES

Taste and see that the LORD is good.
Oh, the joys of those who take refuge in him!
PSALM 34:8

CROOKNECK SQUASH AND ONION

3 to 4 yellow crookneck squash, sliced thin
1 large Vidalia onion, sliced thin
¼ cup butter
¼ teaspoon sugar
½ teaspoon salt
¼ teaspoon black pepper

....

Cook ingredients together until squash
and onion are fork tender. Serve hot.

BAKED SUMMER SQUASH CASSEROLE

2 pounds summer squash (mix of zucchini and crookneck)
1 to 2 tablespoons vegetable oil
1 large Vidalia onion, sliced thin
1 cup milk
1 cup bread crumbs, divided
1 or 2 eggs, well beaten
½ teaspoon salt
½ pound American or cheddar cheese, divided

....

Grate squash and steam in skillet with enough oil to keep from sticking. Add onion, cook 10 minutes; cool slightly before adding milk and ¾ cup of bread crumbs. Add eggs, salt, and half of cheese. Put into baking dish and top with remaining bread crumbs and cheese. Bake at 325 degrees for 30 to 45 minutes. Yield: 8 servings

AMARILLO SQUASH AND CHEESE CASSEROLE

4 pounds crookneck squash, sliced
2 pounds zucchini, sliced
1 large Vidalia onion, chopped
2 tablespoons sugar
1 teaspoon salt
2 cups water
1 cup sharp cheddar cheese, grated
1 cup American cheese, grated
1 stick butter, cut in pieces
1 cup half-and-half

••

Cook squashes, onion, sugar, salt, and water in saucepan for 20 minutes. Drain and mash. In buttered casserole dish, alternate layers of mashed squash mixture and cheeses. Dot with butter and pour half-and-half over top. Bake at 300 degrees for 15 minutes.

CORN PUDDING

2 tablespoons sugar
1½ tablespoons cornstarch
1 cup milk
3 eggs, well beaten
1 (15 ounce) can cream-style corn
2 tablespoons butter, melted
½ teaspoon salt
⅛ teaspoon nutmeg

....

Mix together sugar and cornstarch. Gradually add milk, stirring constantly, until smooth. Add eggs, corn, butter, and salt, mixing well. Pour into greased 1-quart baking dish; sprinkle with nutmeg. Place dish in larger pan with hot water halfway up the side of the smaller dish. Bake at 300 degrees for 1 hour 45 minutes until custard is set. Yield: 6 to 8 servings

CARROT PECAN CASSEROLE

3 pounds carrots, cleaned and sliced
⅔ cup sugar
½ cup butter, softened
½ cup chopped pecans, toasted
¼ cup milk
2 large eggs, lightly beaten
3 tablespoons flour
1 teaspoon vanilla
1 tablespoon grated orange zest
¼ teaspoon nutmeg

....

Cook carrots in boiling water to cover in saucepan for 15 to 20 minutes, or until tender. Drain and mash; stir in remaining ingredients. Spoon into lightly greased 11x7-inch baking dish. Bake at 350 degrees for 40 minutes. Yield: 6 to 8 servings

JON'S GARLIC BACON CHEESE GRITS

3½ cups water
1 cup old-fashioned grits
1 cup milk
¼ cup butter
1 to 1½ cups shredded cheddar cheese
2 to 4 cloves garlic, minced
6 slices bacon, diced, fried crisp, and drained
Salt and black pepper to taste

....

Bring water to boil. Whisk in grits, stirring continuously until smooth. Whisk in milk and butter. Cover and cook on low heat for 10 to 12 minutes, stirring occasionally. Stir in cheese, garlic, and bacon. Cook until cheese is melted, flavors are combined, and grits are thickened. Add salt and pepper. Let sit uncovered for 5 minutes before serving.

ERIN'S CRISPY BREADED OKRA RINGS

¾ cup milk
1 egg
¾ cup flour
¾ cup cornmeal
1 pound fresh or frozen okra, trimmed and cut into
  rings
Oil for frying
Kosher or sea salt and freshly ground black pepper
  to taste

••

Mix milk and egg in a small dish. Combine flour and
cornmeal in another. Place okra rings into milk and egg
mix and let sit for 5 minutes. Then
dredge the rings with the flour
and cornmeal mix. Fry in skillet
containing hot oil
until browned all
over. Do not
crowd the
pan. Place on
brown paper
to absorb oil.
Season and serve.

VEGGIE CHOPPING EFFICIENCY

When you're using your food processor, chop or grate several vegetables at once. Chopped celery, green pepper, and onion can then be stored in tightly sealed bags in the freezer until needed for a recipe.

Quick Tip

BAKED ONIONS

4 cups sliced sweet onion
5 tablespoons butter
¼ cup balsamic vinegar
Kosher or sea salt and freshly ground black pepper
   to taste

Sauté onions in butter until transparent; transfer
onions to a baking dish and set aside. Stir vinegar and
seasonings into hot butter. Pour over onions. Bake
uncovered at 400 degrees for 15 to 20 minutes.

HOPPIN' JOHN

6 slices bacon, diced
¾ cup chopped onion
1 clove garlic, minced
1 (19 ounce) can black-eyed peas, undrained
1 cup rice, cooked
2 teaspoons salt
¼ teaspoon pepper

....

In large saucepan, cook bacon, onion, and garlic until
bacon is crisp and onion is tender. Add peas, rice, salt,
and pepper, and bring to a boil. Reduce heat and simmer
until hot, stirring occasionally.

ROSEMARY ROASTED POTATOES AND PEARL ONIONS

2 pounds new potatoes, scrubbed and halved
1 pound pearl or cipolline onions, peeled
¼ cup extra-virgin olive oil
2 tablespoons fresh rosemary
Salt and freshly ground black pepper to taste

....

Preheat oven to 400 degrees. In a large bowl, toss together all ingredients. Spread in a single layer on a baking sheet. Bake until potatoes and onions are golden brown and tender, about 40 minutes. Serve immediately.
Yield: 6 servings

MOROCCAN PILAF

4 cups rice, cooked
1 onion, diced
1 carrot, peeled and diced
2 tablespoons olive oil
⅓ cup slivered almonds
½ teaspoon cinnamon
⅓ cup dried currants
2 tablespoons orange zest
¼ teaspoon cayenne pepper
1½ tablespoons fresh chives

Keep rice hot. Sauté onion and carrot in oil over medium heat until soft; add to rice. Combine remaining ingredients (except chives); add to rice. Sprinkle with chives and serve hot.

SPICY ORANGE MASHED SWEET POTATOES

3 pounds sweet potatoes
1/3 cup orange juice
1/4 teaspoon nutmeg
1/4 teaspoon ginger
1/2 cup chopped pecans
1/2 cup brown sugar
1 teaspoon grated orange zest
1 teaspoon cinnamon

....

Bake potatoes; cool slightly and mix with juice, nutmeg, and ginger. Spoon into greased 9x13-inch baking dish. Combine remaining ingredients and sprinkle over potato mix. Bake at 350 degrees for 20 minutes or until thoroughly heated. May be made a day ahead and heated before serving.

BUSY DAY
AU GRATIN POTATOES

1 (2 pound) package hash brown potatoes
1 (10.75 ounce) can condensed cheddar cheese soup
2 cups milk
1 small onion, grated or diced
½ teaspoon kosher or sea salt
¼ teaspoon freshly ground black pepper

....

Mix all ingredients and put into a lightly greased 13x9-inch baking dish. Bake at 350 degrees for 1½ to 2 hours.

PICKLED BEETS AND ONION

1 (16 ounce) can sliced beets
½ cup beet juice
½ cup cider vinegar
¼ teaspoon salt
½ teaspoon cinnamon
¼ teaspoon whole cloves
1 small onion, sliced

Combine all ingredients in saucepan. Heat to boiling; remove from heat. May be served hot or refrigerated several hours or overnight.

ZUCCHINI, ONION, AND TOMATO CASSEROLE

2 zucchini, sliced thin
2 yellow onions, sliced thin
2 tomatoes, sliced thin
2 tablespoons olive oil
1 cup Parmesan cheese, grated
½ teaspoon dried thyme
¼ teaspoon salt
⅛ teaspoon freshly ground black pepper

In a lightly greased casserole dish, put half the zucchini, onion, tomato, and garlic. Sprinkle half the Parmesan, thyme, salt, and pepper on top. Add the rest of the ingredients and top with Parmesan, thyme, salt, and pepper. Bake at 400 degrees for 20 minutes.

BETTER POPCORN

If popcorn has been sitting on the shelf too long, it may not pop as well as it did when fresh. Fill a jar ¾ full with popcorn kernels, add 1 to 2 teaspoons of water; put the lid on and shake well. Let the unopened jar sit on a shelf for a couple days. The added moisture content should improve the popping rate of the kernels.

.... **Quick Tip** ....

CORNMEAL MUSH

3 cups boiling water
1 teaspoon salt
1 cup cold water
1 cup cornmeal
Flour for dredging before frying
Butter or oil for frying

Add salt to boiling water. Combine cold water and cornmeal. Gradually whisk mixture into boiling water, stirring constantly to prevent lumps. Cook until thickened. Serve hot.

To make fried cornmeal mush, pour cooked mixture into a well-greased 9x5x3-inch loaf pan. Refrigerate for 4 hours or overnight. Slice, cover each slice with some flour, and fry until golden brown, turning each slice once. Place on brown paper to absorb oil, if necessary. Keep hot before serving.

FRIED GREEN TOMATOES

⅓ cup oil
2 eggs
½ cup milk
2 cups cornmeal
2 cups flour
6 green tomatoes, sliced

Heat oil in skillet on medium heat. Mix together the eggs and milk. In another bowl, combine cornmeal and flour. Dredge the tomato slices in egg mixture and then in cornmeal mixture, making sure slices are well covered. Place in hot oil and cook until golden brown, turning each slice once. Place on brown paper to absorb oil. Keep hot before serving.

BROCCOLI SALAD

5 cups fresh broccoli florets
1 cup raisins
¼ cup carrots, grated
¼ cup red onion, diced
½ cup mayonnaise
¼ cup honey
½ tablespoon cider vinegar
½ tablespoon milk
Salt and black pepper to taste

Combine all ingredients. Chill at least 2 hours before serving.

KELLIE'S DEVILED EGGS

1 dozen hard-cooked eggs, cooled with shells removed
6 tablespoons mayonnaise
1⅛ teaspoons ground dry mustard
¼ teaspoon salt
½ teaspoon black pepper
Hungarian sweet or hot paprika

....

Cut eggs in half lengthwise. Remove yolks and place
in bowl; mash until smooth. In another bowl, combine
mayonnaise, mustard, salt, and pepper. Mix well with the
mashed yolks. Divide the yolk mixture equally among
the egg whites using a small scoop or spoon. Sprinkle
paprika on top; refrigerate until ready to serve. A drop
or two of hot sauce may be added to the mayonnaise
mixture if desired. Yield: 2 dozen deviled egg halves

QUICK CORN FRITTERS

Oil for frying
2 tablespoons canola oil
2 (15 ounce) cans corn, drained
2 cups self-rising flour
½ cup milk
4 eggs, lightly beaten
½ teaspoon black pepper

In large pot, heat oil to 400 degrees. Stir remaining ingredients together in bowl. Drop fritters mixture into hot oil by large spoonfuls. Turn fritters until golden brown. Do not crowd the pan. Place on brown paper to absorb oil. Serve hot.

QUINOA AND DRIED CRANBERRY SALAD

½ cup balsamic vinegar
1 to 2 tablespoons honey or sugar
4 cups cooked quinoa
½ cup red onion, diced
1 cup celery, diced
½ cup dried cranberries
1 cup grated carrot
½ cup slivered almonds

Combine vinegar and honey; set aside. Combine remaining ingredients. Stir well. Serve warm or cold.

DELIGHTFUL SPINACH

2 (10 ounce) packages frozen chopped spinach
¼ envelope dry onion soup mix
½ cup sour cream
¼ cup cheddar cheese, grated

....

Cook and drain spinach. Place in a 1½-quart baking dish. Combine dry soup mix and sour cream; stir into spinach. Sprinkle top with cheese. Bake at 350 degrees for 20 minutes or until thoroughly heated.

RATATOUILLE

1 teaspoon salt
1 eggplant, unpeeled and diced
2 zucchini or crookneck squash, unpeeled and diced
2 green bell peppers, diced
2 stalks celery, diced
2 onions, diced
¼ to ½ cup olive oil
4 tomatoes, peeled and quartered
¼ teaspoon fresh ground black pepper
½ teaspoon dried basil
¼ teaspoon dried oregano
¼ teaspoon dried rosemary

Salt and drain eggplant in colander for 20 minutes. Sauté the eggplant, zucchini, bell peppers, celery, and onion in oil until lightly browned. Drain; transfer to casserole dish. Add tomatoes and seasonings; toss lightly. Bake uncovered at 325 degrees for 1½ to 2 hours.

DON'T CRY OVER ONIONS

Here are some great tear-free solutions for handling onions:

- Keep onions in the refrigerator. Warm onions easily release their fumes.
- Peel and cut onions under running water.
- Don't cut off the "bloom" end of the onion—where the fumes are stored.

Quick Tip

STUFFED BAKED TOMATOES

8 medium tomatoes
4 cups fresh bread crumbs
1 cup mayonnaise
1 teaspoon fresh basil, chopped
4 teaspoons olive oil

....

Cut off the top slice of each tomato. Scoop out centers;
chop and toss lightly with next 3 ingredients. Divide
mixture evenly into each tomato. Drizzle olive oil evenly
over tomatoes. Place in shallow baking dish. Bake at 375
degrees for 20 minutes. Yield: 8 servings

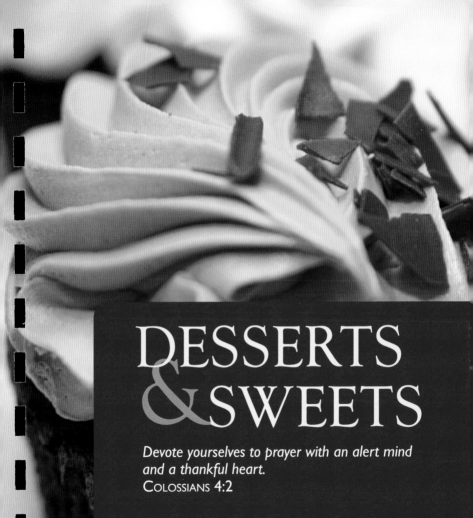

DESSERTS
&SWEETS

*Devote yourselves to prayer with an alert mind
and a thankful heart.*
COLOSSIANS 4:2

COCONUT CAKE

1 package white cake mix with pudding
1 (14 ounce) can sweetened condensed milk
1 (16 ounce) container frozen whipped topping, thawed
1 (16 ounce) package shredded coconut

Bake cake according to directions on box. While cake is warm, punch holes in it and pour sweetened condensed milk over cake. Let cool completely. Combine whipped topping with half the coconut and frost the cake. Sprinkle remaining coconut on top of cake.

CHERRY DELIGHT CAKE

1 (20 ounce) can crushed pineapple with juice
1 (21 ounce) can cherry pie filling
1 package yellow cake mix
1 cup chopped walnuts or pecans
1 (7 ounce) package shredded coconut
1 stick butter, melted
Ice cream, optional

· ·

Preheat oven to 350 degrees. Dump pineapple and juice into a greased 9x13-inch pan and spread evenly. Spoon the pie filling over top of pineapple. Sprinkle cake mix evenly over fruit layers. Add nuts and coconut, and pour melted butter evenly over the top. Bake for 30 to 40 minutes until top is lightly browned. Serve warm with ice cream.

STRAWBERRY FLUFF

1 pint fresh strawberries, trimmed
1 cup ginger ale
2 cups orange sherbet
2 teaspoons honey

In blender, mix ingredients together. Spoon into dessert glasses. Place in freezer until ready to serve.

HUMMINGBIRD CAKE

3 cups flour
2 cups sugar
1 teaspoon baking soda
1 teaspoon cinnamon
1 teaspoon salt
2 eggs, well beaten
1½ cups vegetable oil
2 teaspoons vanilla
1 (9 ounce) can crushed pineapple, undrained
1 cup chopped pecans
¼ cup chopped walnuts
2 large or 3 small bananas, mashed

Grease and flour angel cake or tube pan. Mix dry ingredients; add remaining ingredients and stir well. Pour batter in prepared pan. Bake at 350 degrees for 65 to 80 minutes until pick inserted in center comes out clean. Cool cake in pan. Sprinkle with powdered sugar before serving.

FLORIDA CAKE

1 package yellow cake mix
1 (1.4 ounce) package orange gelatin
4 eggs
⅔ cup vegetable oil
⅔ cup water

Glaze:
¾ cup orange juice
¾ cup sugar

Combine cake mix, gelatin, eggs, oil, and water in bowl; mix well. Pour into greased 10-inch tube pan. Bake at 350 degrees for 1 hour. While cake is cooling, make glaze by cooking orange juice and sugar in small saucepan for 5 minutes. When cake is cool, remove from tube pan and place on cake plate. Poke holes in cake with drinking straw, fork, or skewer. Spoon orange glaze over cake. Yield: 10 servings

LORRAINE'S TEXAS SHEET CAKE

2 cups sugar
2 cups flour
2 sticks butter
4 tablespoons cocoa
2 eggs
1 teaspoon vanilla
1/2 cup buttermilk
1 teaspoon baking soda
1 tablespoon vinegar

Frosting:
1 stick butter
1/4 cup milk
4 tablespoons cocoa
1 (16 ounce) box
  powdered sugar
1 teaspoon vanilla
1/2 cup chopped nuts

Combine sugar and flour in bowl. In saucepan, bring butter and cocoa to boil. Combine eggs, vanilla, buttermilk, baking soda, and vinegar. Combine the three mixtures, mixing well. Pour batter onto ungreased 11x17x1-inch baking sheet. Bake at 375 degrees for 20 minutes; do not over- or underbake. Bring to boil butter, milk, and cocoa. Stir in sugar, vanilla, and nuts. Spread on hot cake.

CREOLE CAKE

2 cups sugar
½ cup vegetable oil
2 eggs
2 cups flour
2 tablespoons cocoa
⅛ teaspoon salt
½ cup buttermilk
1 teaspoon vanilla
1 teaspoon baking soda
1 cup boiling water
1 (12 ounce) can evaporated milk
1 cup brown sugar, packed
¼ cup butter, melted
1 cup chopped walnuts
½ cup coconut

....

Cream sugar and oil; beat in eggs. Sift flour, cocoa, salt;
add to creamed mixture alternately with buttermilk and
vanilla. Mix baking soda with boiling water; add to batter.
Pour into 10x13-inch baking dish. Bake at 350 degrees
for 35 minutes or until pick inserted in center comes
out clean. Mix together remaining ingredients; pour over
baked cake and broil until bubbly.

HANDY CONVERSIONS

Liquids

3 teaspoons = 1 tablespoon
4 tablespoons = ¼ cup
5 tablespoons + 1 teaspoon = ⅓ cup
8 tablespoons = ½ cup
16 tablespoons = 1 cup
2 cups = 1 pint
2 pints = 1 quart
4 quarts = 1 gallon

EASY FRUITY CAKE

1 cup fruit pie filling of your choice
1 box any flavor cake mix
1 cup chopped nuts of your choice, optional
1 stick butter, melted
Scant ¼ cup water

....

Put fruit pie filling into ungreased baking dish. Sprinkle dry cake mix over top. Add nuts if desired. Pour melted butter over top as evenly as possible. Sprinkle water on top. Bake at 350 degrees for 50 to 60 minutes.

OLD-FASHIONED MOLASSES COOKIES

1 cup molasses
½ cup butter
1 teaspoon baking soda
2¼ cups sifted flour
1¾ teaspoons baking powder
1 teaspoon salt
1½ teaspoons ginger

Bring molasses to boil in large pot. Remove from heat and add ingredients in order listed. Chill dough. Roll out very thin (⅟₁₆ inch). Cut into desired shapes. Place on lightly greased baking sheet. Bake at 350 degrees for 5 to 7 minutes. Do not overbake, as the cookies will become bitter.

DONNA'S PEANUT BUTTER FUDGE

2 cups sugar
1 cup milk
¼ teaspoon salt
2 teaspoons vanilla
¼ cup butter
1 cup peanut butter

....

Mix sugar, milk, and salt in saucepan over medium heat to 240 degrees or soft ball stage on candy thermometer. Remove from heat. Add vanilla, butter, and peanut butter, mixing well. Pour in buttered pan. Let cool before cutting.

CHEWY MOCHAS

¼ cup semisweet chocolate chips
1 teaspoon instant coffee powder
2 egg whites
Dash salt
½ cup sugar
½ teaspoon cider vinegar
2 tablespoons flour
½ cup coconut
¼ cup chopped nuts

Melt chocolate in saucepan over low heat or in microwave. Stir in coffee powder. Beat egg whites with salt until foamy; gradually beat in sugar until mixture forms shiny peaks. Beat in vinegar. Fold in flour, coconut, and nuts. Drop by teaspoon onto greased or parchment-lined baking sheet. Bake at 350 degrees for 10 minutes. Yield: 2½ dozen

HELEN'S SUGAR COOKIES

1 cup butter, softened
1 cup shortening
1 cup granulated sugar
1 cup powdered sugar
2 eggs
1 teaspoon almond extract
1 teaspoon vanilla extract
4 cups flour
1 teaspoon baking soda
1 teaspoon cream of tartar

Cream together butter, shortening, and sugars. Add eggs and extracts, mixing well. Combine dry ingredients, and add to creamed mixture. Stir until thoroughly mixed. Drop by teaspoonfuls onto parchment-lined baking sheets. Bake at 375 degrees for about 10 minutes. Do not let these brown. These cookies freeze well.

DIVINITY

2½ cups sugar
½ cup white corn syrup
½ cup water
2 egg whites, beaten stiff
1 teaspoon vanilla
½ cup chopped walnuts

....

Mix sugar, corn syrup, and water in saucepan over
medium heat to 240 degrees or soft ball stage on candy
thermometer. Beat gradually into the stiffly beaten egg
whites. Add vanilla and walnuts. Beat until mixture holds
its shape. Drop on waxed or parchment paper. Yield:
about 36 pieces

QUICK AND EASY ICE CREAM CAKE

1 box ice cream sandwiches
1 (16 ounce) container frozen whipped topping, thawed
1 package chocolate sandwich cookies
1 bottle magic ice cream topping

....

Put ice cream sandwiches on bottom of 13x9-inch pan, breaking into pieces to fit spaces, if needed. Mix together whipped topping with 1 row of cookies that have been crushed. Put on top of ice cream sandwiches. Shake magic topping well and drizzle over top of cake. Freeze until set. Remove from freezer about 5 to 10 minutes before serving.

EASY COCONUT MACAROONS

1 pound shredded coconut
1 (14 ounce) can sweetened condensed milk
2 teaspoons vanilla

....

Combine ingredients. Drop by teaspoon onto
generously greased or parchment-lined baking sheet.
Bake at 350 degrees for 8 minutes. These are very soft
cookies when removed from the oven; let them cool
slightly on parchment before placing on rack. Yield: about
4 or 5 dozen

EASY BUTTERMILK SUBSTITUTE

A combination of ¾ cup plain yogurt and ¼ cup whole milk is a good substitute for buttermilk in a recipe. Another option when you don't have buttermilk is to mix up 1 cup milk with 1 tablespoon lemon juice. Let either substitute mixture sit at room temperature for 15 minutes before using.

Quick Tip

LEMON SPONGE PIE

¼ cup butter, melted
1 cup sugar
3 tablespoons flour
3 egg yolks, slightly beaten
3 tablespoons lemon juice
2 teaspoons grated lemon zest
1½ cups milk
3 egg whites, beaten until stiff
1 prepared pie shell, unbaked

Blend butter, sugar, flour. Add egg yolks, lemon juice, zest, and milk. Fold in egg whites. Pour into pie shell. Bake at 450 degrees for 8 minutes, then at 325 degrees for 25 minutes.

LEMONADE PIE

1 baked pie shell, graham cracker shell, or meringue shell
1 quart vanilla ice cream
1 small can frozen lemonade concentrate
Whipped sweetened heavy cream, optional

··

Prepare pie shell; set aside. Soften ice cream and frozen
lemonade. Combine and mound in pie shell, and
place in freezer for at least 4 hours. Remove
from freezer approximately 10 minutes before
serving. Garnish with whipped cream, if desired.

COCONUT CUSTARD PIE WITH CRUST

4 eggs, well beaten
½ cup self-rising flour
1¾ cups sugar
2 cups milk
¼ cup butter
½ teaspoon vanilla
1 (7 ounce) package shredded coconut

....

Mix all ingredients well and divide batter into 2 lightly greased 9-inch pie pans. Bake at 325 degrees for 45 to 60 minutes, or until a knife inserted in the center comes out clean. This pie makes its own crust.

PECAN PIE

3 eggs
⅓ cup light brown sugar
⅓ cup sugar
½ teaspoon salt
⅓ cup butter, melted
1 cup white corn syrup
1½ cups pecan pieces
1 prepared pie shell, unbaked

....

Beat eggs; add sugars, salt, butter, and corn
syrup. Stir in nuts. Pour into
pastry-lined pie pan. Bake
at 375 degrees for
40 to 50 minutes,
or until filling is
set, watching
that the
pecans do
not burn.

SWEET POTATO PIE

2½ pounds sweet potatoes
½ cup sugar
½ teaspoon nutmeg
⅛ teaspoon cinnamon
1 teaspoon vanilla
¼ cup butter
2 eggs, beaten
¼ cup evaporated milk
1 deep-dish 9-inch pie shell, unbaked

Boil sweet potatoes until tender; drain, peel, and mash well. Blend in sugar, spices, vanilla, and butter. Fold in eggs. Add milk and beat until fluffy. Pour into pie shell and bake at 300 degrees for 35 to 40 minutes, or until lightly browned.

PUMPKIN PECAN PIE

3 eggs
½ cup sugar
½ cup brown sugar, packed
1 tablespoon flour
½ teaspoon salt
½ teaspoon nutmeg
½ teaspoon allspice
1 teaspoon cinnamon
2 cups pumpkin puree
1 (12 ounce) can evaporated milk, heated to lukewarm
1 deep-dish 9-inch pie shell, unbaked
1 tablespoon brown sugar
2 tablespoons butter
¾ cup broken pecans

....

Blend together eggs, sugars, flour, salt, and spices. Mix in pumpkin puree; then gradually add milk. Pour into pie shell and bake at 450 degrees for 10 minutes. Remove pie from oven. In a small saucepan, melt remaining brown sugar and butter; stir in pecan pieces. Spoon over pie and bake at 350 degrees for 40 minutes more.

CHERRY SQUARES

½ pound butter
1 cup sugar
1 teaspoon almond or vanilla extract
2 eggs
2 cups flour
1 cup chopped walnuts or pecans
1 can cherry pie filling
Powdered sugar, optional

....

In a large bowl, cream butter and sugar; add extract. Stir
in eggs, one at a time. Mix in flour and nuts. Spread ¾
of the batter into an ungreased 9x13-inch baking dish.
Cover batter evenly with pie filling. Drop remaining
batter onto filling and spread. Bake at 350 degrees for
45 minutes. Let cool, cut into squares, and sprinkle with
powdered sugar before serving, if desired.

PEANUT PIE

1 cup dark corn syrup
3 eggs
3 tablespoons flour
2 tablespoons butter, melted
¼ teaspoon salt
1 cup whole peanuts, shelled and toasted
1 prepared pie shell, unbaked

Combine syrup, eggs, flour, butter, and salt in bowl. Beat for 1 minute. Spread toasted peanuts in bottom of unbaked pie shell. Pour liquid ingredients over top. Bake at 350 degrees for 30 minutes.

FRUIT CRISP

4 cups fruit (peaches, pears, plums, quince, or berries)
½ cup sugar
2 tablespoons cornstarch or flour
2 tablespoons lemon or orange juice
½ cup rolled oats (not instant)
½ cup flour
¼ cup brown sugar, packed
2 tablespoons chopped, toasted walnuts or pecans
6 tablespoons softened butter

....

Preheat oven to 375 degrees. Lightly grease a 1-quart casserole dish. In a large bowl, mix the fruit, sugar, cornstarch, and juice. Spoon into the prepared dish. In the same bowl, mix the oats, flour, brown sugar, and nuts. Cut in the butter until the mixture resembles coarse crumbs. Sprinkle over the fruit mixture. Bake for 45 minutes, or until lightly browned and bubbly.

PEARL'S COCONUT CAKE

1 box yellow cake mix
1 pint sour cream
1 ½ cups sugar
4 cups flaked coconut, divided
4 ounces whipped topping

Bake cake in layer pans according to package directions.
Cool completely. Split each layer horizontally to make 4
layers. In large bowl, mix sour cream, sugar, and 3 cups
coconut. Set aside 1 cup of sour cream mixture. Spread
remaining mixture between cake layers, stacking to make
a 4-layer cake. Combine reserved sour cream mixture
with whipped topping. Spread over sides and top of
cake. Sprinkle remaining 1 cup coconut over entire cake.
Cover and refrigerate for 3 days before cutting.